The Footprints Of My Life

MICHELLE GRIFFIN

© 2021 Touched By A Dove Publishing

Michelle Griffin

The Footprints Of My Life

All rights reserved. No part of this publication may be stored in a retrieval system or reproduced in any form, or by any means — electronic, mechanical, photocopying, recording, or otherwise — without permission of the publisher or in accordance with the provisions of the Copyright, Designs and Patents Act 1988, or under the terms of any license permitting limited copying issued by the Copyright Licensing Agency.

Published by: Touched By A Dove Publishing
Text Design by: S. Michelle LeSuer
Book Editing by: Dana Hutchinson
Cover Design by: Tanisha Pettiford
Cover Photo by: Jackie Griffin

A CIP record for this book is available from the Library of Congress Cataloging-in-Publication Data

ISBN-13: 978-1-7355336-6-7
LCCN: 2021925069

Hurt, pain, loss, loneliness, fear, disappointment, sadness…. I leave you on these pages. You have been evicted….your lease on my life is over.

~ Michelle ~

Dedication

I dedicate these footprints of my life to my angels in heaven…my Jackie, my Mommy, my Daddy, my Aaron, my Sonny, and my Yvette. I know you all watch over me. My heart cries when I think of each of you and my missing you is indescribable. I know I walk amongst angels, sent here by God to fill my life with love.

My earthly angels, Tierra, Jackie, and Alexis, I dedicate this work to you also. My heart overflows with love for you and I know I am favored because God saw fit to let me be your mom. I am incredibly proud of all three of you and my cup runneth over because of you. You are my greatest joys.

Contents

Family Over Everything	1
Fearfully & Wonderfully Made	24
Butterfly Kisses	30
Who Are We?	36
Matters of The Heart	49
My Heart Cries	57
It's Hard to Say Goodbye	68
2020	79

Family Over Everything

Momma

The hardest thing I've had to do
Was to say goodbye to you

To watch you slowly fade away
To see the sunlight leave your face

To sit helpless as you became so weak
Frail, Unable to see, unable to speak

To see you try to keep a smile
As life slowly slipped away
To see fear in your face, in your eyes
The unspoken words you couldn't say

I prayed to God to help you heal
To take this suffering away
Always believing he would do it
Just wouldn't do it my way

I know that you needed to go
So the suffering could end
But I was reduced to your little girl
Because I had lost my mommy, my bestest friend

Momma
You were my favorite girl
Losing you
Changed my entire world

I'll never forget that awful day
How I longed for another moment, just one
But the stallion had come for you
Just like that, tomorrow would never come

I'll never get to run to you
Tell you all my fears
I'll never get to hang with you
Now, I have to wipe my own tears.

Why did my biggest fan, my sweetest peach, my feisty queen, my Georgia girl
Why close her eye for the last time
And leave me alone in this cruel world

To question God, why linger there,
I know it is all his plan
Why do I keep asking why
Why try to understand?

Just know our God is faithful
Know Our God is true
I know He knew it was time
He did what was best for you

I miss you so much more than my words could
ever say
So often I still cry for you,
I'll always love you, Mrs. J.

Let The Good Times Roll

He taught us to stand tall
To be strong and be proud
He made us feel like royalty
Made us residents of clouds

He showed us the finer things
He made sure we finished strong
He loved us hard, he loved us stern
He taught us right from wrong

He told us life was for living
To enjoy every single day
He never stepped into a church
But he told us Jesus was the way

He believed in a good time
Bowling, Fishing, running dem streets
Always rooting for them Skin
From his special season seats

He lived every day as he wanted
Everybody loved the man of gold
He worked hard, he played hard
He Let the Good Times Roll

No, he wasn't perfect
Far from it, we all knew

But our Daddy was our hero
Despite the things that he would do

There definitely was no denying
He was the best Daddy around
We worshipped where he walked
Thought it was holy ground

Couldn't tell us he wasn't the best
Our Big Harold was the man
Always there for every event
He and mama, our biggest fans

Yeah our big dude was something
A treasure to behold
And he never missed a moment
To let the Good Times Roll!

Jackie

Plucked from my life too soon,
Just a baby you and I
47 long years later
And still my broken heart cries

You were my best friend,
The pain I felt the day you left
Forever fresh, forever in my mind
Taking a part of my heart
But leaving a part of you behind

I promise I will never forget you
I celebrate you every year
Making sure your nieces know
The Auntie Angel is still here

I know you're smiling down on me from heaven
Helping me make it through the day

Willing me to press on
Guiding me through the darkness
Showing me the way

I know I have a special angel assigned to me
You and God whispering to me
To believe I am fearfully and wonderfully made

Reminding me I can do all things with Christ
I am clothed in strength and dignity
I am a child of the King

I know you guys talk about me
Willing me to be strong
Pushing me to use my gifts

To show the world I am a survivor,
I have overcome

I think about you often
I miss your gently face
Our long talks, our little walks
My praying you would be saved

I carry you with me
Heaven's flowers, Gods appointed
You live inside of me
Forever growing, blooming
Heavenly anointed.

Pssss...

Sigma man, what it do
you sure look good in that Sigma blue

Hop in the car, let's take a ride
To the Mecca on the yard
I promise I'm good people
Trust me, I got you, I'm a Sigma sweetheart.

March 3rd, 1984
The day you took a chance and got in
Who knew that after that day
You'd become my college boyfriend.

Long talks, late night walks
Kissing and carrying on in my ride

The love we shared grew so fast
You proposed before a new year arrived

Getting married really young
Twenty six and Twenty seven
Before we knew it there they were
Our very own gifts from heaven

3 precious little angel girls
Sent for us to raise
Trial and error, doing our best
While giving God all the praise

The months turned into years
Time moved on so swift
Never forget that despite it all
You were one of my greatest gifts.

Psssss…..

Never Knew A Love Like This

As I looked into your eyes
A tear welled up in mines
How God must love me to give me you
Such a diamond, so beautiful, so rare
You were here and I was immediately in love
I never knew a love like this

You were so perfect, so beautiful
You look at me and I melted
You touched places inside my heart I never knew existed.

I would protect you with my life
I would love you with all my heart
I would teach you, show you God
Be all you needed me to be
Through me, God had produced life
A beautiful child who would bring me sheer joy
You were my Ms. America
My T-Bird
My everything
I never knew a love like this before.

Beautiful Soul

You carry the spirits of my sisters
You bear the names of them too
You changed my very world
I see so much of me in you

You carry your aunties strong will
Both of them were something else
Very much like you
Confident in themselves

They did their own thing
Either get on the train or get off the track
Beautiful Soul your just like that
If you ain't wit me, step to the back

You walk to a different beat
Making moves and doing you
Sassy, Sexy, Smart, and Feisty
Carry a little Mrs. Jones too

Your gonna change the world
Taking chances, living dreams
Using God's gifts as a gateway
Busting through traditional seems
Just looking at you melts my heart
You are one of my biggest joys
I was blessed with the best of the best
Forget about baby boys

Jackie O, without a doubt
A Black Girl who Rocks is who you are
A diamond in the rough
One of God's Superstars

The world had better get ready
You took lemons and made lemonade
Devil tried to stop your progress
But You are Fearfully and Wonderfully Made

I got my pom-poms and my horn
You know the loudest shouts will come from me
Go change the world Beautiful Soul
I am cheering for you eternally

Miracle Child

They said it couldn't happen
It was too risky
I couldn't do it

Who are they?
Who gave them the final say?
God was in control

Against all odds, I journeyed
Taking precautions all the way

Praying
Waiting

Believing
Afraid yet strong
Determined

I believed in miracles
God had saved me for such a time as this
Amongst many witnesses

You burst into the world
Strong, Loud, and Beautiful
Our miracle
My Miracle
A Miracle Child

Aaron

Some days my heart cries for you
My mind is filled with thoughts of you
Silent tears spill from my eyes
I can't believe you're gone
Can't believe it's true

You were our little song bird
My lil girl, their sister too
You come to our minds so often
As we reminisce about chilling with you

God brought you to us
You quickly penetrated our hearts
Singing songs, telling stories
Disney movie were the favorite parts

Looking out for Chuchie
Like it was your assignment from above
Making sure Jackie and T were always OK

Showing us unconditional love

I still look for you, listen for you
You silently slipped from our lives
Often times I sit alone and wish for you
As heartbreak tears leave my eyes

Aaron Ashley, gone too soon
I should have come to you
I was too late
You were gone, slipped away
And this mother's heart still breaks

I pray you know we loved you
And that will never change
I pray you know we will never forget
Our lives will never be the same

Gone too soon
Gone from me
Gone from us
Gone

Sista

When God felt the time had come,
in the midst of calamity
It's like my world was frozen in time because
there you were, standing in front of me.

I couldn't speak a word,
I couldn't believe it was true
It was like looking in a mirror,
but I wasn't looking back, it was you

As questions filled my mind and
my heart raced with uncertainty
It was as though a weight was lifted from you,
secret exposed, finally free

So much to say, so much to learn,
so much wasted time
God had finally answered an old prayer, you
weren't just any sister, and you were mine

The bond that we would share,
formed long before that day
Neither of us knowing the strength of it,
created by God and miraculous faith.

Growing together in grace,
putting differences aside
Not allowing circumstances to define us,
letting love be our guide

Moving step by step, day by day,
as we shared what lies ahead
Looking forward, never back,
making new memories instead
I thank God for giving me you,
best of friends, sista girls
I love you, baby sis,
thanks for entering my world

Brothers

Big Brother, the leader of the pact, the one who took flight, who journeyed from home, singing a different song

An adventurer, one who I'd change nothing about, created to be different as you swish through sawdust across the floor to an unfamiliar country song. A song about a STAR, who shines bright in the northwest night

Always using your gifts to help those no longer able to help themselves, while all along sometimes needing a gentle hand to guide you through. Strength and pride define you, making you the Boss you were born to be

My blue brother, my one time, two times, three times I know you'll always love me, brother, even when we don't often say it. My ABLE brother, my creative brother, building, molding, modeling, shaping, growing, making mountains out of molehills…A scholar and a gentleman

My Sigma brother, the blue blood that flows through our veins doesn't define us but it binds us…forever connected

My baby brother, the namesake, the youngun,
growing up different but raising to the top,
proudly shaking off obstacles, making moves,
defining your own destiny, doing the damn thing
The fireball who will fly from zero to 1000 in no
time flat but if you need him, he also will always
have your back. Dog lover, climbing high making
things happen in the sky, Quiet thunder, small
wonder, loving those who love him back

Smooth Brothers, cool brothers, a blessing from
God brothers, my brothers, Jones brothers, Damn,
I got the best brothers

Valley Girls

Growing up in The Valley

Like a neighborhood used to be,
Real life-long friends
I look out for you, you look out for me

Back when people used to care
When your neighbors were your peeps,
Don't let them catch you cutting up
They'd tear you up in them Valley streets

Neighborly love was really a thing
People cared about each other,
Disrespect was not accepted
I feared your mother and my mother

Fathers were at home
We all grew up real tight
Come for us if you wanted to
Better be ready for a fight

Valley girls were close-knit
Hanging tough, being cute
Chasing fellas in red Nova's
Up on Larchmont and at the pool

Standing on the corner
Talking trash and waiting on the early night,
Knowing we had to book
When we saw the damn street light

House parties in the basement,
All of our friends from school,
Slow dragging in the corner
Girl, you know the light was blue

Hanging with our Valley brothers
Making sure we all were good
Making sure intruders knew
We from the Valley, yep that's our hood

Growing up and graduating
Life taking us to different places,
Moving into adulthood
But never forgetting familiar faces

Never forgetting Valley love,
Valley families, Valley girls,
Never forgetting our Valley
Where we had the best of all worlds

Fearfully & Wonderfully Made

Time Stand Stills

When the setting sun touches the quiet seas
And the day separates from night
Time stands still

When cool breezes dance across your face and
darkness surrounds you
Speckles of sparkles light up the sky
Time stands still

When God whispers to man......Behold the beauty
of my work
Embrace the magnitude of my wonders
Time stands still

Know that I am God
That I cause the sun to set and the moon to rise
That I molded earth just for you
That I make time stand still

Find peace in my sovereignty
Joy in my quiet moments
Serenity in the moonlight
Know that I make time stand still

Love Letter to God

Dear God,

This is your child, your servant, your creation

Thank you for knowing my name, for loving me despite my many faults

For saving me from dangers seen and unseen

For forgiving me for the seemingly unforgivable

For being my peace in the midst of my many storms

For ordering my steps, guiding me, carrying me

For constantly reminding me that I am fearfully and wonderfully made

That I can do all things through you

God, I thank you for saving me when disease tried to devour me

For strengthening me when life tried to deplete me

For picking me up and telling me to rise when the

battle in my mind tried to
defeat me

For whispering in my ear and penetrating
my heart when depression and anger tried to
dehumanize me

Because of your love

Now I am stronger……I am Wiser……I am Better

Because you never gave up on me and you never
let me give up on me

Thank you for delivering me, for fighting my
battle, and winning.

Whispers From God

Silent thoughts, gentle whispers, unexpected blessings
Wild bunnies that gather at your doorstep
White doves that visit you in the morning
Whispers from God

Unexplainable coincidences
Dreams that have slipped from your mind into your reality
A gentle breeze, wildflowers
Whispers from God

Butterflies that flutter about, rainbows where there's no rain
Unspeakable joy, unwavering faith
Healing….overcoming…deliverance…miracles
Whispers from God

Unbelievable phenomenon, unmistakable encounters
Undeniable blessings
All
Whispers from God

Grant Us

God grant us simple pleasures
Unspoken moments
Little joys
Rainbows
Sunshine
Snowflakes and rain
Blooming flowers
Butterfly kisses
Agape love

Butterfly Kisses

You

Like dew in the morning
You gently rest upon my heart

You occupy my thoughts,
You take control of my dreams

As the sunlight causes the buds to bloom
You seep into my soul and cause
My mind to whisper your name

Even when I try to fight it
Memories of you slay me and I smile at the thought of you

My heart races when I speak your name
My body trembles

You are my cherry on top
My winning spin, my knight in shining armor

You are my gift from God

You are my you!

Summer Time

The sun is hot, the days are long,
and the DJ plays your favorite song
Summer, summer, summer time
Time to sit back and unwind

Sassy sandals and sundresses,
swimming pools and parks
Paddle boats and funnel cake,
loving the beach moonlight after the dark

Late night strolls, holding hands,
the skies light up with stars
Carnivals and Ferris wheels,
turtle wax on all the cars

Family reunions, bar-b-ques,
playing spades with your peeps
Summer concerts, eating crabs,
playing football in the street.

Road trips and round trips,
spending family time with the crew
Sling shots and drop tops,
make it do what it do

Summer love, all booed up, roses blooming all around

Lightning bugs and butterflies,
caterpillars on the ground

Ice cream man, Rita's ice,
watermelon hits the spot
80, 90, 100-degrees,
man does it get really hot

Summer, summer time,
my favorite time
Time to sit back and unwind.

Music

Rescue me and take me in your arms
Rescue me and fill me with your charms
Can't you see that I'm lonely
Rescue me

Restore my trust in love
Let your dreams be my dreams
Let the music penetrate my heart
Like a cool and gently breeze

Take my hand Alpha man,
Lead me to the Promised Land

Sing my favorite song
Make my fears
Float, Float, Float, float on

Be my dream maker shawty
Let me be your Mary Jane
Be the sunshine of my life
Love me like you've gone insane

Sing me a 70's love song
As we hand dance to Frankie B
Slow dragging to Sarah Smile
Let Marvin take us to ecstasy

Why don't we make music together
My lyrics, and your beat
Music that speaks to the soul
Like Teddy, Mary J, and Smokey

Let the music take control
Like quiet whispers to your mind
Butterfly kisses to your ears
Quiet storm on rewind….

Who Are We?

Sunshine

Your smile brightens my day
It's blinding and enticing
Your energy brings joy to the room.
You are a genuine jewel
Who brings light to those around you
You love deep and the children are your
Pride and joy
You teach from experience
Implanting wisdom and knowledge
Into the mind of the youth

An authentic butterfly who wraps her wings
around the world
Depositing bits of sunshine
You rise up like the sun
And find beauty in simple pleasures

Your eyes dance with sun rays
As God spills words of affirmation from your lips
You are like a summer breeze
That dances across my flesh
Planting sunny butterfly kisses in my mind

You are beautiful, inside and out
Funny, caring, and kind
You are my sunshine

Survivor

Say it isn't so
There must be some mistake
I am a 30-year-old woman
Not a senior saint

This doesn't happen to the young
Surely not to a new mom
God would never give the ultimate blessing
Then throw me in a storm

Infiltrating ductal who
What in God's name is carcinoma
I think you have the wrong patient
I am a young, brand new momma

Hold on, slow down
Surgery, chemo, radiation too
We had barely reached 30
We had no idea what to do

Sitting in disbelief
Crying silently in shock
My whole world turned upside down
I was run over by a Mack truck
So you mean I'm gonna die
I won't get to raise my girls
No one will love them like I do

Who's gonna teach them about the world

Oh my God how could this be
How would I ever endure
You're saying I have breast cancer
Look again, are you sure

In total fear and disbelief
For 3 days I cried and cried
Then Yolanda Adams said
this battle ain't yours
Give it to God, fight girl,
and survive.

So we all began to pray
Told the doctors do what you do
We are not bowing down to cancer
We had so much more living to do

The journey was unexplainable
The pain and suffering seemed forever
Family and friends rallied around us
Taking turns, holding my family together

Slowly through each treatment
Six months of chemo, 6 weeks of radiation
Lifelong side effects
And permanent disfiguration

I found my voice, I wore my badge
Pink ribbons everywhere
Telling everyone who would listen
Breast cancers not a death sentence
But a stepping stair

God blessed me to live
To raise my girls, to survive
27 years later, no new cancer
Still healthy and alive!

I Am a Queen

Hey Black man, I am a Queen
Treat me like nothing less
Shower me with your love
Handle me with tenderness

Honor me with your words
Respect me like you know you should
Compliment my sexy curves
Love me like only you could

Protect me at all cost
Walk beside me not ahead
Never harm me with your hands
Wrap me in your arms instead

Don't leave me in the dark
When you retreat within yourself
Talk to me, come to me
Don't put my heart up on a shelf

I was created just for you
Rib of your rib, bone of your bone
Meant to share in your world
Not to sit silently alone

I'm classy, cute, and confident
Independent, beautiful, and strong
I'm fragile, emotional, and moody

I'm the words of a love song

I love hard, give my all
Combine your dreams and goals with mine
I am driven and determined
I am definitely one of a kind

My smooth brown skin will entice you
So will my soft brown eyes
My soft lips will plant butterfly kisses
You'll find pleasure between these thighs

My heart will burst with tenderness
I'll touch places deep in your soul
I'll crown you king of my world
My love will drip on you like pure gold

When our spices blend together
And our bodies become intertwined
My heart beat will match yours
Stolen moments, lost in time

Yeah Black man, I am a queen
Royalty through and through
I was created for a purpose
Molded by God just for you

I'll protect my rep at all cost
Sometimes I'll stumble but won't stay down

I'm a survivor, a super woman
I proudly rock this queen crown.

MICHELLE GRIFFIN

Don't Crook My Crown

America, we are Kings and Queens
Descendants of Royalty
A unique gift from God
A precious commodity

My original ancestors were not slaves
But Kings and Queens of distant lands
Being shackled, beaten or sold
Couldn't have been part of Gods plan

We were created to rule
To honor God, to be free
We were not created to worry or fear
But to live in harmony

Who told you we were the enemy?
You got the game so twisted
We tried to help you win the battle
Your ignorant ass just missed it.

My Black brothers are not criminals
No more than any other race
Don't accuse them of heinous acts
Because of the color of their face.

Why do I need to show my I.D.
When your brothers are not required
Why do you blame our President

For the mess that you conspired

Don't label my children as slow
Because they learn differently
Don't assume I'm ignorant of the law
Because your badge gives you authority

Don't follow me in stores
Assuming I'm a threat to your goods
While you waist time watching me

The real threat, your friends, wear hoods.

Ahmad was hurting no one
Trayvon was just a child
Garner was a gently giant
You brutally murdered Michael Brown

Don't put your knee in my neck
Choking me until I have no breath
Then expect me not to be mad
And exercise my right to protest

We are so tired of this disrespect
We've had enough, you went too far
You bullied us one time too many
You could have left Saundra in her car

We've stood back angry and mad
Trying to wait for justice to prevail

Instead of justice, just more deaths
And now the cities burn like hell

Well guess what, evil people
You oppression didn't hold us back
Mae Jamison, Thurgood Marshall and Barack Obama
All those American Heroes Black

See we are a praying people
And we know God will bring us through
We press on, we keep trying
Believing in Him, not in you

We making moves changing lives
No matter how much you try to put us down
No matter how much you show you hate us
You don't crook our Black crowns.

A Man

A man who is gentle
A man who is patient, and who is kind
Who's genuine and trustworthy
Who doesn't play with my mind.

A man who knows God
One who will pray and worship with me
A man who puts me first
A man who knows I am a queen

I want a man who is strong, a sexy man
One who is confident and bold
One who's adventurous and spontaneous,
Being his girl never gets old

A man who will push me
In a swing at the park
Moonlight walks on the beach
Cuddling on the sand after dark

One who caresses my back
As he looks deep my eyes
One who tells me I'm beautiful
And that he's such a lucky guy

A man who knows my worth
Who will hold me when I cry
One who won't judge my faults

Or break my heart with constant lies

A funny man who makes me laugh
Who takes me to exotic places
With a swipe of his true love
All my fears and pains….erased

I need a man who truly loves me
A man who will receive my love too
A man who will share my dreams
Is my fantasy man you???

Matters of The Heart

Love

To love and to be loved is to feel the sun from both sides
To find joy in simple things
Sunshine ….. Raindrops …….Snowflakes
Love has no limits…..
when you feel loved
Iridescent rainbows shoot through the skies of your heart
Morning dew caresses your thoughts
Causing excitement to drip from your veins
It's like butterfly kisses all over, awakening your very senses
When you find love, it's like honeysuckles in springtime, sweet and succulent
Love is kind, love is giving and receiving.
Love is precious
Love is sowing and reaping
Love is love…agape love, brown suga love, deep love….
Be kind to it, be there for it
Don't neglect it or disrespect it
Because love needs love
If love don't live there anymore
Love will find love
Because love is in love with love

Young Love

I remember when I first laid eyes on you
Oh yeah, that dude is fine
Before the season is over
This cutie pie will be all mine

I played hard to get
You played the same game too
Although I couldn't stand your arrogance
I also couldn't stop looking at you

You asked for my number
Matter of factly, I gave it to you
Deep inside I was excited
Couldn't wait to spend some time with you

Never admitting I was afraid
What would you expect of me
Four years of age between us
Would I be what you needed me to be

Inseparable from the start
Growing tighter every day
Having fun, falling fast
You became my everything

A teenage love affair
Destined to never stop
Falling for the first time

The first giving of my heart

Brand-new feelings, new desires
Never felt this way before
Is this it, have I fallen
Who's this guy that I adore

Does he feel the same way too
Is he also on cloud eleven
Is Brainstorm singing to us
When they say "This Must Be Heaven"

"Always and Forever",
Each moment with you
It's just like a dream to me
That somehow came true
Is it all a dream
Could this type of love be real
He smiles when he looks at me
He has to feel what I feel

I smile at the mere thought of him
Just wanna be where he is
Just wanna be in his arms
Wanna feel his tender kiss

As we gaze in each other's eyes
And never want to part
A feeling so difficult to explain
A gentle tugging at my heart

Spending late nights together
By the water at the park
Holding hands, making plans
Kissing like grown-ups in the dark

Growing up so fast, believing love would never end
Two hearts now beat as one
He became my lover and my friend

As Larry Graham serenaded us
A one in a million love
The always and forever kind
Sent from heaven above

Bowling alleys, amusement parks
Miniature golf, were our things
You the Cowboys, me the Skins
Man, the battles that would bring

Life was simple, love was strong
Four whole years we were together
Everybody, including us
Thought our love would last forever

But fate had different plans
A different path our lives would take
Young love came to an end
Two tender hearts would break.

As I look back on that time
Even though you struggle to recall
I remember my young love
Yeah man, I remember it all.

First Time

Tonight's the night
So excited yet so afraid
This changes everything
There's no turning back
Tonight I take the step
Tonight I give all of me
Tonight I leave being a little girl behind

My heart beats so fast
My mind races

I don't know what to do
Tears well in my eyes
Are you sure...
Am I sure...
You know I...
You know this
You Know...
Yeah baby, I know...
I love you and I know...
Trust Me
Hold Me
Don't Cry...
I got you...
Oh my God.......
Oh MY GOD.......
A single tear rolls down my cheeks
I've changed!

MICHELLE GRIFFIN

You See Me

In a crowded room
People moving all around
Music blaring, lights flaring
You see me

In a darkened space
Can't make out a single face
But you see me

Through plastered smiles, a façade, a lie
Living inside for fear I'll begin to cry
You see me

Shadows in the dark, past mistakes worn like a
garment....invisible
Yet, You see me

Moving on through life
Pretending to be free
All the while ignoring
What's right in front of me

Joy is on the other side
Peace in within my reach
Forgiveness spills from my lips
Happiness is calling
You see me

My Heart Cries

MICHELLE GRIFFIN

Loneliness

Loneliness is like a vice
It grips you, smothers you
It walks you down a never ending path
A path you walk alone

Trying to imagine it's not really there
Trying to convince yourself you'll be fine

You are never alone the saints say
You've always got Jesus
He will comfort you, be with you
You hold fast to that thought
You make it your thing
You tell yourself, this too shall pass

Then you see it…..a couple holding hands
Walking, talking together, laughing together….
Reality hits

Jesus is in your heart but who is in your arms
Jesus walks with me and talks with me
But who holds my hand
Who can I feel
Jesus speaks to my spirit
But who speaks my name

I got Jesus deep down in my heart
But my body has deep desires as well

Loneliness leaves you broken
Searching desperately to replace it
New adventures new responsibilities
New task, new people

You try to keep busy, stay active
Don't let it control your mind
Don't let temptation crowd your thoughts
Be strong, be wise

But loneliness is strong too
It will eat at you like a parasite
Haunt you like a spirit
Ride you like the wind
Devouring.......Diminishing
Discouraging
Dissolving your very strength
Loneliness

Do I Ever Cross My Mind

Do you ever think of me
Do I even cross your mind
The way you used to love me
Is that love forever lost in time

Forbidden footsteps, unchartered waters
We should have never entered in
The price I paid was way too high
Lost my heart, lost my friend.

We shared our biggest secrets
Talking hours at a time
Suddenly the talking stopped
Do I even cross your mind

We knew it wouldn't be forever
SO much wrong from the start
Stolen moments, silent treasures
Should have been more careful with my heart

Just wasn't built to be alone
Built for sunshine in the rain
Built to share my heart, my dreams
Built for compassion, for love, for man

But as loneliness surrounds me
Silent tears streak my cheeks
The strong woman fading

Deep inside, I just feel weak

As I sit alone in the darkness
Months gone by without a trace
Willing thoughts of you to leave my mind
Get out my heart, just hit erase

How I wish it were that simple
Forget the memories, forget the time
Instead I sit silently and wonder
Do I ever cross your mind

MICHELLE GRIFFIN

Let It Go

I can't hold on to the pain
It's blocking the sunshine and the joy
I can't keep letting it rest in my heart
I want to feel the love
To walk in freedom from the past
I want to be whole again
I gotta let it go

I want to not let it win
I am stronger that this, I know
I want to not look back at it
There's so much more life to live
There's so much more to give
There's so much more to do
I have to let it go
My blessings are being blocked
They can't get by the wall
I'm stuck in a peculiar place
Breaking the Shackles
Freedom

I can't breathe
I'm drowning
I'm suffocating
I gotta let it go

No one can save me but me
No one can turn it all around

No one can make it right
I hold my future in my hand
But it's smothered by my past
I gotta let it go.

I'm trying
I'm pressing
I'm praying
I'm moving
I'm walking away

Let It Go

Free

Stuck in a lonely place
Unable to escape……Trapped by my own thoughts

In a room filled with people……..Yet feeling all alone

Do they see me
Do they know I exist

Darkness surrounds me
I fear life, I fear death
I feel like giving up

I cry out ….God I need you
Take my hand, pull me back to life
Don't let me dry up and die

Guide me out of darkness Lord
Command the elders to pray
Our Father, who art in heaven
Hallowed be thy name

Water me so I can bloom again
Strengthen me so I can fight
Breathe on me so I can feel joy
Forgive me so I can be free.

Twisted

How the hell did this happen
We both knew better from the start
Keep it simple, keep it casual
Don't let any of this touch your heart

Infrequent sightings, morning hellos
Much debating and conversing was the plan
We stopped paying attention, being careful
And it all got out of hand

Don't let it out, keep it silent
Maybe the feelings aren't real
Maybe if you never say it
Somehow you won't feel what you feel

You know it's all a set up
A disaster in the making
Act like you aren't falling
In other words, keep faking

But you find yourself wanting more
More than he can ever give
Secret lovers aren't consistent
They have to protect the life they live

So now you are perplexed
Damn it, your fragile heart went too far
You gotta retreat, get out of this

This thing is affecting who you are

Now you feel so weakened,
Even mad, feeling rejected
Wanting more, getting less, all alone
Seemingly neglected

Ok that's it, I'm done
I gotta quit before I break
Walk away, you'll be fine
That's all your heart can take

It was forbidden from the jump
Should have kept yourself as friends
Secret love changed everything
Now everything has to end

So say goodbye, close the chapter
This is how the story ends
I didn't make it a full day
Before missing you entered in

Now what do I do
The song you sent is on repeat
My favorite artist, words penetrating my mind
I had no idea you felt this for me

Blindsided by those lyrics
You always acted to unaffected
So the song made me see some things

I totally never expected

Damn slim, you got me twisted
Missing you is tougher that I thought it would be
I lay awake at night wondering
Am I alone or is he also missing me

It's Hard to Say Goodbye

Moving On

One of the hardest things to do
Is to let your children go
To allow them to move on in life without you
To mature, to grow

To no longer be their confidant
The one they turn to when they need love and affection
To no longer feel like you hold the space
Of a source of guidance or direction

Having them pull away from you is heartbreaking
Simple conversations so hard to have
Feeling like you are always intruding
No longer hanging or sharing laughs

My girls have always been my world
My road dogs, my American Express
Now our lives have changed
I watch from the sidelines at best

To let your little girls become women
And no longer settle all their situations
To realize you must step back
They don't want you in their private relations

Apprehension and confusion
Trying not to step over imaginary lines

Just don't say anything, ask no questions
If they need you, you aren't hard to find.

What a difficult reality
For a mother, learn to let it be
But I guess it's all part of the plan
They've grown up now they have to make their own history

I will always be here.

I Had to Save Me

There is no turning back, the damage has been done
I had learned to accept anything
But this was the forbidden one

Tragic memories, childhood fears, I had buried them deep within
Praying never ever to surface, never to have to face them again

Now it was my turn, history had found my door
That fearful life I had lived as a child, no longer buried any more

Those fearful nights of hoping he would stop
Please don't hit her this time
Just leave like you often do
When you leave we will be just fine

Go Daddy, just go I begged through my tears
Oh God, there it was, the demon had appeared

As I sprinted from my bed, running to my brothers' side
Crying, screaming, God where are, come on yall, we gotta hide

Run, momma run, oh God, are you there

We'd hear her screaming as he hit her, she must
have been so scared

Scarred for life believing, the open wounds would
never heal
How could the man we loved so much, how could
any of this be real?

I live in love and in fear of the only man in my life
I wonder if I'd have to live this way
Was this required of a wife?

Now it was my turn, history had found my door
That fearful life I lived as a child
The life I vowed I'd never endure

I would never live that life,
my 11th commandment it would be
I'd never put my girls through that
No man would ever put that fear in me

But demons have no preferences, they will slip in
without a clue
That demon slowly took over my second man and
there was nothing I could do
After years of forgotten love, years of praying and
trying to renew
One December afternoon, it happened, the demon
had control of you

Out of anger, frustration, rage, and out of the blue
My life changed forever from a single blow from you

All the pain came rushing back all, the memories of the past
I felt myself breaking, I had to leave and leave fast

As I became an enraged monster, Black woman mad as hell
How did this shit happen to me, no way I could go to jail.

I was living my history, the forbidden line crossed in the sand
I'd never be same, not for him or for any man

I felt like I was drowning, trust became a memory
No amount of prayer and fasting, could possibly bring me back to me

Nervous, anxious…always looking for an attack
No resting, no joy, always watching my own back

I tried to block it out, tried to move on, to forgive
Tried to say it was only once, I had a good life, let it go…live.

Apologies, counseling, tears or time, nothing seemed to work

I believed he never wanted to hurt me, but my
shattered heart was broke

I had to make a move, I couldn't live in fear
I couldn't always wonder if the demon lived in
there

I had to save myself, so many didn't understand
or agree
But they hadn't lived what I lived… I had to go
save me!

When Forever Ends

As I sit here in silence
No words pass between us
Like strangers in the night
The atmosphere is so empty
Yet the space between us is so small

Silent days, lonely nights, going months at a time
Wondering what really happened
To the love you promised was mine all mine

Did that love die, disappear, fade away without a trace
I lay her empty, dead to love, only sadness fills my space

So many years, now like ships passing in the night
Only darkness between us, nor words, not more fight

This couldn't be my life, this couldn't be what God meant for me
What happened to joy, to happiness, to living the American dream

I guess we didn't pay attention, busy being parents, living life
In the midst of all of that, we forgot to be husband and wife

So much emptiness fills the space where your love
used to reside
I wear it like a mask, no longer able to hide

How can you mend a broken heart, time will tell, I
guess
How do we start all over, do we find happiness

Time we can't get back, I hate the path we took
You'll always be my guy, even though we've
closed the book

I'm not bitter, I'm not mad, God bless us both I
pray
There are parts of my heart that will be yours....
forever and a day

Goodbye

I lay awake in silence
Trying hard to comprehend
How did we make these mistakes?
How did we lose sight of what is right
How did we let forbidden love enter in

Two separate thoughts became one
Clouded judgements, intertwined
Caution thrown to the wing
Boundaries forgotten, now undefined

Despite how hard I tried to ignore it, tried to pretend it wasn't real
There's no way this could be happening
No way I could be feeling what I feel

Shake it girl, retreat
Disaster lives within those thoughts
Don't let loneliness treat you like a puppet
Guard your feelings, protect your heart.

Walk away from this situation
Just be strong and let it be
Everything will be just fine
Let it be a memory

But then the unexpected,
Blindsided by a simple song
Smokey whispers hidden truths
And what was right not feels so wrong

Ecstasy and agony, secret lovers lost in time,
Quiet storms, OOO baby, baby,
Being with you altered my mind

You occupy my quiet thoughts,
Repeating the song, revealing things I never knew
I lay awake, unable to rest
I try, but I can't stop thinking of you.

What's it all about?
How did your life blend with mine?
How did we let careless whispers change our very minds

And now I try to walk away,
Try to do what's best for me
But inside I just feel broken,
Unsure, alone, and weak.

So, I cry out to God,
Please guide me through
My world is cloudy, my heart is open as I try to say goodbye to you.

2020

MICHELLE GRIFFIN

Pandemic

Like a meteor that crashes into the earth
A sing bolt of light creating destruction
Devastation, physical and biospheric mutilation,
Ripping us of life

The pandemic crashed on earth's surface
Spreading like wildfire,
consuming us
Infecting the air, threatening our very existence
A catastrophic situation that took over the entire nation

Unprecedented, unheard of, unimaginable
We were trapped, trapped inside
Unsafe to go out, confusion all around
Our leaders let us down.

No one knew how to fight it
Warnings were ignored,
Thousands of people dying
Everyone turning to the Lord

The world was on lockdown
People scrambling for necessities
Toilet paper, sanitizers,
Lysol spray, and groceries.

No entry without a mask
Virtual learning for all school
Curfew and mass closings
We were governed by new rules

Fear of exposure made us crazy
Inside was the only safe place
Wash your hands, sanitize
For God's sake don't touch your face

Many months of quarantine
No outside family, no friends
We thought we were coming out of it
And the cycle starts all over again

The book of Revelations come to life
Pestilent, pandemic, and distant clouds of smoke
COVID 19 came to take the world
And the repercussions were no joke

People lost their businesses
No income, no work and no food
Seemed like God had had enough
And there was nothing we could do

But in the midst of terror
Threw the worst catastrophe of our time
People who normally relished the thought
Recognized it was praying time

Families bonded together
Virtual church services were so packed
People learned to help each other
Learned to actually have each other's back

Family dinners became a thing
Taking walks in the park to exercise
Telephone calls to check on loved ones
DJs rocking the house on Facebook live

Yeah, despite fear and death all around
During a time of quarantine and lock in
Jesus whispered to his people
Follow me, I am Love,
And Love always wins.

2020

As we rang in the New Year
We had absolutely no idea
A catastrophic world pandemic
Would consume the entire year

We were unprepared and unequipped
To handle such devastation
We had planned vacations and staycations
And all kinds of celebrations

Then as we did not pay attention
Cause the warnings were all there
Across the ocean from China
COVID 19 landed here

It was as if the death angel
Traveled from door to door
Killing family members and friends
Those we love and adored

We had no way to fight it
A science fiction movie scene
We kept wanting for it to end
To wake up from the bad dream

Then without justification, a reason or a cause
A white cop in broad daylight
Lynched a black man named George Floyd

Civil unrest began, Black Lives Matter was the call
Black America had had enough
Time for racism to take a fall

The entire world joined the protest
Police brutality had to stop
We had reached the breaking point, Hard to trust any cop

2020 was something else, a year of turmoil and distress
The whole world was flipped upside down
Simply put, it was a mess

Cancer

Even cancer has to bow down to Jesus……
PERIODT!

About The Author

Michelle Griffin is a proud Prince Georgian. She grew up in Pleasant Valley in Seat Pleasant, Maryland with her lifelong friends who she is very much in touch with over 50 years later (#PV4LIFE). She has been a community servant throughout her career serving as a teacher in P.G. County for 22 years. She is a devoted member of New Chapel Baptist Church and serves faithfully with the Top Ladies of Distinction, PGCC and the Powerful Divas with a Purpose.

Her biggest joy are her three beautiful, talented, amazing daughters who she affectionately calls her American Express Cards, she doesn't leave home without them. This Black Girl Who Rocks loves hanging with her girls, her sister, Lisa, her handsome brothers Andre, Tim, and Harold and all of her teacher friends.

Identifying as a lifelong learner, she holds a Bachelor's Degree from University of Maryland, a Master's Degree from Bowie State University, and is currently pursuing a Doctorate Degree from American College of Education.

Michelle is an avid supporter of breast cancer awareness, and gives God all the credit and praise for her 27 years of survivorship of the disease. Her favorite scripture, Philippians 4:13, I can do all things through Christ who strengthens me, defines how she lives her life. Nothing is too hard for God!

You can contact Michelle at perfectpraiz1@yahoo.com for speaking engagements, book signings, or to encourage breast cancer survivors and their families.

www.ingramcontent.com/pod-product-compliance
Lightning Source LLC
Chambersburg PA
CBHW071908070526
44583CB00016B/1904